Hello and thanks for your support. I am Belinda L. Sears and I have been writing since my 7th grade year in middle school. This is my first published book. I am from a small country town, Enfield, North Carolina. I have always love to write to inspire others, my family and me. Writing helped me to cope with my circumstances in life. This is my collection of poems and inspiring words of encouragement.

Gaining Momentum, Into Bees World

by Belinda L. Sears

Raleigh, NC

Table of Contents

WINDOW

As people come and go I wonder who they know? Where's they going and who's their people? Do relatives know they are always here in this terminal as they come and go. Believe me they do not know. Every day the same old ones comes up to the window and asking for something. It doesn't make a difference what it is: mask, holders, schedules, pens, paper, spoons, or money. All freebies they want from me. Some want attention, to talk, to joke or laugh and just have fun. Others want a girl, woman or a man, its funny cause some want none. Some just come to look, others come to show off their clothes, while others are wearing holes. Some are dirty. Some are clean. They all want to hang around and lean right in front of you, thinking of ways to approach my window. Some come to use the bathroom. Some make a bathroom on their own. Some want to touch their nose and hand you some. Many leave their possession around being in a hurry and expect it to be there when they call. They get mad at their own fault. Some get posted on the wall, some are not allowed to ride the bus at all. Some want to argue even get angry, others want to be left alone. As the buses goes in and out, some miss their bus and won't to shoot, some stop and think, I missed the bus because of me. Some pushes fake babies in a stroller, while some walks a skateboard as a dog with a cord. Some look on and never reply. Some looks over and laugh until they cry. Always look to your left or to your right but don't never stare, things are happening everywhere in this place and I see it all in one designated place from my window.

I LOVE HARD

When I love, I love hard and now I'm scared but spared! On to the next love I will find by being open minded and kind, yes now and later. I tell myself, "I will not let my guard down to a clown that frown or bow down to what could be fake as the date just to get the bate".

A piece of ass to carry your way just to say "dam its good". So you decided to come back knowing it's not slack. Good and tight, that's the way it should be. When I love, I love hard crazy me.

Crazy me for thinking, you were the right one for me, never again. You held my hand, we took walks in the park, and you kissed me gently. You held me close it brighten my day, yes I admit, it wasn't supposed to end this way!

I'm in love that's all I can say, sorry you just felt another way. Slayed! The day I was made, from the crest of my breath, to the hole in my chest. Carry on your day, you didn't fit into my life anyway, crazy me I say; from the start I told you "when I love, I love hard".

NO ONE TO BLAME

No one to blame, no one to blame! The one to blame is me. After all these years of being alone, no one to blame.

I wanted a new beginning, no one to blame. I met this guy and felled in love. The love of my life, no one to blame.

I was committed, I gave and gave my all, no one to blame. Things began to get rough, no job or money only bills piling up. No one to blame.

I worked overtime to make it right. We don't have to give up nothing because I got you with all my might. No one to blame.

Habits became a problem, alcohol, drugs, and cheating! No one to blame. You step out of line in time and now you even wanted to come back. No one to blame.

Sure, I missed you dearly, no one to blame. I supported you still every step of the way. No one to blame. I let it go with all the years we spent. No one to blame.

I offered my friendship, it wasn't good enough! I cut you off. No contact at all. I feel good, my mood is great. There is no shame because it is no one to blame.

A SHAME

An introduction about this guy, were all I needed to say good-bye. Man oh man outstanding as usual, ring out in time. Good and awesome conversation were mine. I started to love him and accepted him into my life. Shared with him the importance of me. Always on the lookout because his journey will be, even though it didn't include me. Distance we became. A twist of mind was apparent. Living life on the edge did nothing for me. To run around for nothing and could not see. You got to be crazy or is it me?

WHAT DID YOU SAY

What did you say? What did you say? Why are you whispering? I can't hear you. What did you say? You talk to fast. Please slow it down, I didn't understand, what did you say? You know you heard what I said, no I did not. An argument, I took no pleasure in one; outburst arose one after another and some. Why are you getting so upset, what did I do to you? What did I say to get you so fired up? Nigger please!

Please don't turn your head on me, why are you walking away? What did I say? Please do sit down and stay. No! I am gone, but why? Are you coming back, yes it was said but in the heart I knew it was bad. So I reckon it will be another day.

Why do you question me? When you don't understand nothing I say. Explain myself to you, I don't explain myself to anybody but I am not nobody! Somebody I am, hello! What did you say and why are you doing things this way? You didn't say.

THIS GUY I KNOW

This guy I know, I thought I knew him well. I was hoping that he was real. As I pierced deeply into him, it was all fears and tears. This guy I know, I thought he was really funny, it turned out he's a bunny; jump, jump, jump here he go again. I use to laugh so hard at his jokes, now I choke.

This guy I know, he talked really smooth; only to get me in the groove. Yes! It happened and it was really cool. Awesome!

Later, this guy I know and thought he was very cool, turned out to be a big fat fool. When I smile, he smiles; then he wilds out only to see if I shout. No anger, no sorrow, and no lashes back, just to see if he would fall through the cracks. The cracks of knowing what he was doing really so, man I had to go.

This guy I know, have no fear of what I could say, he was a bad boy on any given day. It was more than eyes could see if he wanted to be with me. I say catch up, catch up before I go. I'm on my way, it will be nothing you could say.

This guy I know love to talk smack, I listened well as I put him on a rack. A rack of bricks, he was full of tricks. I just know it shows, I only wished this guy was a bush because he would be mushed.

Yes! I found this guy I know but I didn't know him well as I tell this story I think of his lying as tale, this guy I know.

WAIT FOR IT

Wait, wait, waiting for the phone to ring. Wait! Wait, waiting for a text. Waiting for an appearance. Waiting for a drive by. Waiting to let go. Waiting for something to happen that day! Day after day, week after week and month by month past. Wait for it, wait for it and wait for it.

IT FINALLY STOPPED

Thank you, thank you, thank you! It finally stopped. The female robin left me alone. She had taunted me enough. I'm glad I said and thankful she's gone. No more knocking or pecking on my glass door, window and siding at all times of the day and late evenings. Yes, she had knocked so much I had to get comfortable with it and I left her alone. Okay, I admit yielding to her; now she's gone! I said only if I had a BB gun, she would've been gone a long time ago. She left me something behind to remember her, a stinking mess! Her drippings all over the place. I asked myself "why me". Just like humans every breathing living thing loves to get their way, she got it, yes she did. What bad timing it was for me. Next time I will be prepared. Let me clean up this mess this robin left behind. I looked up. there she goes; okay it finally stopped.

WATERS BE STILL

Down in the water of this crazy mixed up world, where the people laugh and cars honks as they pass by; live a people of all sort of the masses from the so-called greatest to the down low on the total pole nasty. Johnny and Mary are their names, I'm sure you have heard of them but it's never the same. Love at first sight as I could recall. The two of them was so high and on a rim not relatively small. The whim was turning and they both could see, intrigued by each other as the last apple on that one old tree. As Mary reached up to take the first bite, Johnny was right around the corner in plain sight. The two arms extended and true love begin as they both grin and now sin is in the wind. Let's go sit down we will talk in unison. It was a beautiful day, sunny and bright covid19 were in our very site. Little did they know, how near or far; it was here! They never forgot that particular day, it went surpassingly well to say. Yes, we made it through that day; waters be still!

A NEW BEGINNING FOR ME

Yes! It's a new beginning for me, now it's one! I can embrace and enjoy me. I can find peace beyond compare, live without surrendering a wasted thought, a monetary donation, a toxin relationship, a stalker and the nagging of a child.
A new beginning is what I planned out to have, I wanted it. I need it and I will get it. Now it's mine, no looking back, no catchers caught, no mending or bending; open air is what I'm breathing!

I will be the sun rising until the sunset. I will be shinning bright as the star at night. I will go and come as I please. Eat, sleep and rest without any pest. I will make my day and my night, everything I do will be out of sight.
Only me I will depend upon, which sounds pretty and awesomely good. I will have no doubt as some may think I should, doubt causes confusion which I eliminated. See, it's time for me a new beginning.

DOGS IN MY NEIGHBORHOOD

The dogs in my neighborhood, I can see all, big ones, little ones, and medium ones. There are black ones, brown ones, light brown ones, grey ones, white ones, and mix color ones all in the neighborhood. There are tall ones, short ones, one leg ones, no eyes ones, and no tail ones too. There are ugly ones, pretty ones, long haired ones, short haired ones, no hair ones and even young, old, and no eyes ones, all sorts of dog in my neighborhood.

As I sat on my front pouch, I'm going to tell you this story about these dogs in my neighborhood. This is real and straight to the point, sit back and relax as you see the many dogs that I see. Dog lovers is exactly what it is, never a dull day. It will have you in dismay. At present I don't own a dog, as I watched them walk their dog I wished I had one with me.

The dogs in my neighborhood is a site to see every day. Day after day, I see all these dogs going their way. Pulling the owner one by one whether it's in the sun, rain or snow these dogs are always on the go. Busy, busy, busy is what I can see as they sniff around on the ground looking for the scent to squat. Poop is what they do, now scoop it and take it with you. Most do, some don't and now at times when you walk by the smell is in the air. Come on now. We all got to care. The dogs in my neighborhood.

THE BLACK CAT IN THE NEIGHBORHOOD

It's a big black cat in the neighbor, that roams around. He goes from one pouch to the other looking and lurking to see what it can find. I don't know his gender but it acts like a male cat. Why I say that? He loves to hang over at my house. He protects my domain and I thank him all the same.

House to house he goes, to see what's going on. I can see him laid out on someone's lawn. This is no ordinary cat. He's amazing as he traveled up and down the street. He greets all the people he meets, welcoming them to the neighborhood. When I moved in he was the first one I saw, he welcome me too.

This cat scared me so bad at first, yes I was afraid of him, always sneaking around. You never knew when he would appear, I would say where is he? Oh my dear! No, I never was a lover of cats and I still don't care for them at all.

The stares he gave me and I gave it back. He would lay under my car, walk on my fence, hide in the bush and at night he would sleep in my favorite chair on my pouch. I never see him much now but I know he's there, because he leaves behind his thin hair. When you see him, you will know, he's that big black cat in the neighborhood for show.

THINGS ARE CHANGING

Things are changing, I can see. Right before my very eyes can see, the trees that were bare now have full grown leaves. The flowers that popped up way too early hung in there, ready for the warm weather to appear. They have the prefect bloom, standing tall not even wanting to fall.

Up in the sky, I can see the birds have begun to come back home. There are some all alone, to take their place and to bask in the sun. Many are flying in open-air as they all play as one. All sticking to the flock as they go around before coming to the ground.

The ants have opened its doors to make themselves known, in which I can't stand. This wonderful creature has opened its home. You better watch out, they are always busy. Don't stand in their way do it will be you to give in that today.

The spiders have creeped out to claim their lot. Web by web, it catches whatever goes by, the spider determines whether it lives or dies. Be careful if you are out at night if it catches you, you would be in flight.

The bugs are on the prowl and the snakes are making their way in the dust. They both hoping to see the dawn of a new day, can't you tell how fast they move to get in their space away from your place!

People come out from hiding, now they are fixing and repairing all the things broken. Grass cutting, planting gardens, pulling weeds even cutting trees. Everyone is hauling things and being smart about their business. And look there are the children on a mission to find whatever is hidden. I watch these things from my front pouch, sitting and looking at all. Things are changing.

IT WAS YOUR TURN

It was your turn. If I could have told you what I knew
before, would you be clinging and clinching? Would
you be knocking, ringing or running to my front door?
Ahead of the game you say and you might be, but look
I'm doing good and you are free. If you could have
looked around, you could have seen how wonderful
things could have been with me. Look now because the
one thing you once saw, have now turned into three.
Time tells all and no! You were my wakeup call. Yes!
You can say you took your turn and you're burned
thrown away for a turn.

THIS IS THE DAY

This is the day, I let it all go. All the pressures that running to and fro. I never wanted to hide the way I see this world that I know outside. On a stage all my life, I just wanted it to be alright. Deep down inside I have pushed it all aside and now I wonder where did it all go. This adventure I wanted so much to pursue, is what's going to make me new. New in a way I must have felt all along but in the past I just blew. Picking up the pieces to start all over, yes 50 now it's nothing undercover. As I walk out this day, a day long to remember of how I caught me and save me from all the tremors. To look straight forward to these exciting days to come, in which I know it will be there, so here I come with open arms, I'll be reaching, embracing the only one, my mom! To share with her the things of long ago a promise. The promise we made and encounters that fades, now on track to bring back something new on this day. I only hope it want be late because we all have our fate. Let me hurry along today it's still young, growing to this babe. Clearing my mind as I past the time, pondering, seeking and reaching into a world I left behind. This is the day my experience will take me away. One to be looked on and upon only to share as an example because this is the day I let it all go and its done.

IN THE RAIN

My heart is broken, yes it has been cracked for a moment. Now it's time for it to mend back again. How long will it take? I don't know but for show it will not go back there anymore. I'm all alone facing the world with only my words of shadow. I'll be the one in the background applauding for everyone else, always staying to myself. As I reach over and get in front, it will happen one day, but for now, I'm just in the shadows finding my way. A way around people like you. I gave you my new beginning, you took it, made it what you wanted to be for you. I'm lost for words right now, time changing and this you know to be true for me and you. I hope to see you in another eye, where you will be dead in a sense of your own ways, that very change will bring you back alive in my eyes. For now, I'm in the shadow I once knew not so long ago at peace and I'm free. Seek me not or seek me at will turn the corner and a shadow will appear, when in the rain I will become so clear a shadow in the rain.

IN THE AIR

Waiting, waiting for the words I wanted to say, somehow he made them all go away. I was stun to him, captivating and admired I were, in the palm of the hand that only had one plan. A plan I knew but wanted it to be true. Grasping for air and longing for love, I kept it going for a while, then I was through. I never forget that day. The day I wanted to jump in his arms, in my bed and be blown away but now he's dead. Dead in the sense of laughing as he went away. I watched he laughed, grinned who's to say. A joke to him, my heart just stopped. I wanted him so bad, it dropped. It wasn't a joke many folks believed it but deep down I knew he must have felt something more too. Circumstances permitted him to leave under false pretenses he pleased, now he's gone and I wondered was it really so. I will never know away he go. My heart still beats strong today for that someone who had gone, in the air.

MY POPS

My pops a sensitive man, a man I enjoy and wanted to know more. I have not always had my pops around, he was gone for 38 years, and bound. I lost him for a time but now he's found. How much more could I learn from him. He's my tree that stand for all eternality, to me you see. My pops, a caring man, a man I adore. He makes me smile all the while I could be crying inside. When I feeling bad, down and out he's always there and not too far away. All my questions he answers, never brushing me off, always letting me know I'm the boss. A man who knows how to talk and relate to a simple me, I thank him so much how he had amplified and enlighten me. My pops have always been well- groomed handsome man. Professional in all he has done, bringing to a table a spread not for only him but more than a few. Great ideas and a plan is what he has and now I have it too. A hard working man who uses his mind to get things done, don't get mad at him you go and get you some. He never set back or run, he challenges himself, using what it is, what might have been, and the now together to make it happen. Most of you might not understand but this is not for you but his plan! A woman's man is what he is, good on the eyes, great in his walk, beautiful smile, nice height and weight I thought; my pops.

GOOD CONVERSATIONAL PEOPLE

Where are the good conversational people? I am looking, and I have not found. I turned to social media years ago, wanting of a good well meaningful simple conversation and I have not found it. I have searched through many different sites. I got on facebook looking and soon found out that its addictive, but I knew me if it's not working I will leave it. I joined many social groups even came up with some of my own; there were no good conversational people anywhere. I supposed it really determined how one think not all are good but the good stink. In my mind there have to be people who would participate in something good if they could relate. It was hard, it's a new era. People like me have been brushed aside, no cause to participate and the others were trying to follow the trend that is why all this began. The old and the young is now playing the same song, it nothing that differentiate them until someone like me come along.

A MAN BEYOND WORDS

He was a man beyond words, the sweetest thing, I have ever heard; from the top of his head to the tip of his big toe, he was my man, a man on the go. A man who would love me and no one would know, I'm surely keeping him and the rest can go. This man ran to me and I to him with a warm embrace in a parking lot where no one could trace. It was the most beautiful sunny and bright day. Our eyes were filled with the radiant of light all for each other and who ever were insight. Our words went rolling down from our eyes through our mouth, in the wind it hit us both in the face and we grinned. In that very moment we had written a new song that was imprinted in our mind and heart that very minute. Yes! A man beyond words.

STOP PLAYING

Stop playing, I say. Who's playing? You are; I'm not on this ride, and I'm getting off. No! You say, what you are doing to stop it? Stop playing! Tricks are for kids you know, I'm an adult. Stop playing! You said "for what, I would see". I have seen, there is nothing to see. Your action speaks with me you see, so stop playing.

POPS, MOM AND ME

Pops, mom and me went for a walk, one early morning. We came across all kinds of people who were walking, even ones who were walking their dogs. We walked up hills and down hills, on flat grounds too. It was a joy to see the three of us walking along the road and conversing with each other. It was fun, priceless I say, we were drawing the attention of some that day. Pops and mom went right along even though the walk was long. I will never forget that day, for the joy it brought to me became an extension of my love for them, which swelled my heart in every part to know the smiles was there because of me. We walked and walked until the sole of my pops shoes start to crumble, first the left then the right, mom and me was through. We laughed and laughed as pops kept up with us both, he started out walking like a pimp, to walking with a limp. Even though my pops did not give up, he was determined and away we go. We kept going until it all dropped off. Yes, we had some fun with my pops until he was done! I cut our walk short and we made it home, my pops, mom and me.

TWISTED

Today's world is twisted. People twist every and anything. The world has lost the need to show love, give freely and respect. In today society of generations, we can stand among authority and still get no respect. Respect is gone. Admit it people, it's down the drain and never coming back. It's not being taught to the young or the older ones of today. You can tell when you met them in the street, on the job and even in the dark. They will look at you and pass you by, if you try to speak, they might ask you why or indicate to you don't try. Respect can't be brought. We are now all here trying to make up a reason for why twisted as they are.

TRAPPED

Yes, trapped. I'm trapped, not you but me. Let me make that plain, so all can see. I'm seeking ways to make things better all along, digging deeper at the deepest until the morning comes. Now I'm all stressed out, not to no ends but all about searching to mend. Holding on to strings gauging and waging until all is dead. Just as a puzzle drops to the ground, I'm looking to make a rebound. I'm not trying to score one or two more just to open another door. Sit down please and allow me to slide by you, because at the end you would have wish you had, but now you mad. Picking up my lips and my smiles, I'm seeing my life as a great big pile. Come on people and stay for a while. The pile so heavy, I can't move; I know when I'm done, but look here come another one who want some. Yes, I said it, how about you? The more I seek, the more I find the way to end this unpleasant day. I'm sitting here all alone writing this way and now you call! If you think I'm talking about you, well you may as well be trapped too.

LOOK

Look at the words we speak now, means very little in this world around. To be spell bound, living in a mound, going round and round as we go. Action usually speak louder than words ever could, but now look at the hood. The hood of the many words we see and hear. The hood of doing things just because we can, seem to me unclear. We lost what we could have had, station yourself now in your pad. You looked to the media for entertainment and gestures no doubt, wake up all people, its only lectures, you heard it from me. Lectures to take you out, make you feel good or important to some in a type of way. Listen to your friends and not see another day. Listening to this poem there is no guessing or dismay, be array in your dealing today about the way you feel. Let's start with ourselves, by spurs of the moments in life, you can really enjoy. Share it with your family, friends including kids or someone else who sees your bids. If time, money or resources is your problem take it from me, handle it and solve quickly. As we began to stand with and for other action, never look over and say or think you are the attraction. You will be fooling yourself, so straighten up and live. Look!

JUST ANOTHER POEM

Just another poem, listen to what I have to say in order for you to take a seat and stay. You beat me. You cheated me. You used me. You took from me. You left me. You smiled at me. You laugh at me. You waved at me. You never said you love me. Yes, you beat me in the games you played, but I lived to see another day. You cheated on me by the promises you made every day it's okay. You left me because business is more important you say, I never did see any money, but who care anyway. When you were smiling at me guess what I was smiling too, those smiles carried me through. You laughing at me, and I'm laugh at you, believe me, we were both laughing too. You waving to me as you pass me by, look at me now see how I can fly, away. I was never able to choose you but still, I saw something in you. You cheated on me, yes its true I always knew and now I cut you off. Enough is enough don't you think. You used me to get what you wanted, I counted it as a lost. I recall what my great grandma use to say, never give out more than you can stand to lose on any given day, so what; it's a lost not for me but for you. Today, you take me as I stand with no demands. Remember, this is another poem. At last you are listening to what I have to say now be on your way.

WE COULD'VE HAD IT ALL

Not a day goes by, I don't think of you. As I see, we could've had it all because we had a ball! I stopped in my tracks, don't want to be held back, but I longed to move forward. Pushed a side each and every day, wondering why he wanted to stay. Begging and pleading to become part of me, my life. Just one positive step toward having the perfect wife. The one you can call, depend on and know she will always be there. The one to comfort and morn with you. The one to see you carry out your mission and be there for you. Rearranging my life to fit your life in, the one guy I will always love from within. Great times we had, conversations were not bad. Your crazy jokes, laughter and weird sounds were all so clear. I miss it for being near. Peace be with you, I'm on my way once more to celebrate a new and prosper day. We could've had it all, I must say. May you always have a bright and sunny day as your sunshine walks away today.

BECAREFUL OF WHAT YOU ASK FOR

It never seems to amaze me about what people say. The answers I get, I just drop my bottom lip. This one time I surely regret. Let me into your world; let me know what's on your mind and then forget. A simple topic of sharing information.

HOW TIME FLY

How time fly. It's my turn to fly bye. How many times have I asked why? I realize it's a good thing to say bye. The life I live, I lived to enjoy, because I cared for so many more. I extend my hand to all who came wanting, wondering and couldn't get it right, life seemed so far out of sight. I have a great big heart, if you ever got to know me, you would say it's true but for those who didn't that's alright too. Sorry you never knew it, now I'm leaving you. Don't morn, frown, cry or say a good bye but look for me on that day, I will be there, you know why. How time fly is my good bye.

BEEN THINKING

I been thinking about you. You, you, and you, are you surprised? Of course not! You are in the present of a queen. It's a perfect day where all thing will be okay. Write this on your walls, ceilings and in your concrete, because this life will never be repeated. You aren't surprise, you been thinking it too.

THE WORLD

What? What have happened to the world I used to know? I don't know but here I go. This might seem stupid or just out of place to think of a world I once knew have now been misplaced. Some might say it's old fashion, even dumb on my part, I would rather be out of this world than to be ripped, tried, searching, and complaining when nothing is being done. Look at yourself, because what I know none will make it through: hold on to this fast pace and let me take you on this ride, I hope it will shock someone deep down inside. The traditional values have lost its place, set aside in some unknown place, more money have been spent than you or me will ever see in this world today. While you and you are running around being misled by someone's else misfortune relationship, looking to gain only by being tortured in fornication. Rules are being broken, morals disappearing every day. Hearts are torn and families broken too, while moms, dads, grandmothers, grandfathers, sisters and brothers are watching from afar. Little can they do and little they made know, it happening more than we can think but still some may seem to glow. How is it that some may ask, let me catch up on what I think, I have come know.

You remember years ago when everything appeared to be getting better, were out of control, you all sit back on your pouches, in your chairs, swings and at your tables pointing fingers as if no one knows. Discussions we all had, decisions were made on those days in our house about where we go from here. Now we all say, I care: some dare to mention this silly me. We could have done more or just do what we could; our generation would have stood. One against the other and yet we all interact. Question? Really something is not right, that was the time to wake up my people and see! We did it with only words, we all held on, as far as we could think or looked back. Confusion we are, many will not confess, because they themselves didn't see this coming now it's a mess, and here to stay.

Everything I known have been touched either in a positive or negativity way, don't matter much, because we live in a world that don't care about such. As I look at each and every one of you, it's disgusting because it's not new. Life seem to repeat itself. The older I get I can see it too. Now I am writing these words to say to you, if you don't stop, greater things for you can be few. I'm 50 at the time of writing this to you, glad to be here conversing with you; if you knew my story you will tell me to get out of here.

It's a shame when you can see what's happening today and why it just don't make sense to me, I'm telling you why! A big game is being played. We are in it together. Many will look at the now, factor to see their way. Some looks at the future and see no hope in today. I looked at the past to bring me up to date because I know there will be a world that will not go. If I see it or not maybe one of my offspring will bring it to the light.

As I sit, I can recall what my great, great grandma said to me, all these things will pass away. She has long gone, I'm here to carry it on. Stop, think what I'm talking about, take heed because it's happening to you. You can sit there like you don't know or get off your butt and go. You have children don't you, I have four. I love them so much more than you will ever know. Prepare yourself for what's in-store. Put your seat belt on tight and we will ride this wave for some days and nights. Please everyone be safe until we meet again, inside another world where we will be waiting for it to begin.

BACK IN TIME

Somewhere back in time you became a friend of mine. The sun was high in the shy. The moon reflected so brightly at night. Where peace made to be still and the blooms opened it mouth, as the scent encircled the air. The vibe of joy was in the wind as it blew gently across both me and you. It brought forth laughter and smiles that no one could compare. Our rest was made not in a day or two, seasons followed and broke through. As I reflect on the path it led, I bow my head not in sorrow but with joy. Now on to the next tune back in time when I met you.

WALKING ALONG

As I where walking along today, a thought came to my mind I can say. It was pleasurable, it brought me to tears without any fears. As I laughed in a silent mode, I began to giggle as if someone else knows. Looking around with a great big smile, I decided to set down for a while. I took notice of the wide open blue sky in it the sun was shinny making the clouds smile. Another smile for me, you see somehow it followed me. I got up, on my way as I turned the corner there was this man wearing green. I never been attracted to green before until this day. He looked at me and said you have come to play; no it's just my smiling day. On my way up the street there was another man dressed in blue. He asked me do I know you? No you do not, I'm only smiling because of a thought running through my head and as for you, there are no reason to dread. It's funny how I have attracted these two men, determined I am, this day is mine! I said within this grin. As I continued down the street, there were an older, well season lady looking out the window with a peak. I throw up one hand and never skipped a beat. I went to the end of the street and stop, now I'm bent. Laughing and smiling in silent mode, as I go. I started to walk at a fast pace, I glance up in this great big tree, there were a young boy stuck, yelling come and help me! I stopped, are you okay? I'm scared please help me down he said. I helped him at that very second. The little boy was glad. We both shared a smile. There it goes again another smile just for me. The little boy said to me "I'm glad you were walking along. It was your smile that attracted me to you. Many pass me I hid from them. You're a special person and I know this to be true. I have observed you a long time as you been walking through. My mom and me stay right down the street. She has always wanted to meet you, I'm here to see that she does meet you". Huh! We see you walking along with a smiling face as if it's painted on your face and keeping a steady pace. My mom not allowed to come out anymore, she's shut up inside and can't come out the door. This is only way she's able to see you now, from a window she peaks through from inside. I'm asking you please come to my house and greet her at will, she would like that, she watching you still. Yes! I followed the little boy back to his home. I felt at ease for I knew my smile would be radiant upon me and on you. Smiling and talking as we walked up to the door steps of his house. There I stop and we heard a drop. The little boy ran inside and never came back. I left that house with a smile. I never got to know why these things happened to me. I knew the little boy meant well, he was at peace because of me. The smile that came upon my face was no ordinary smile. I was so happy until I was dying inside. You all know what I mean, don't act like you don't. Dying in pure joy, brought many smiles on that one day. To stand here now to share with you all, because of a thought that came to mind, as I was walking along; now smile!

FRIEND

Who really are your friend? You were different from the first time I met you, not in a bad way. A handsome guy full of love and compassion at the same time. I myself beauty surround me and sexy followed were all could see. We both had nothing to hide, living life to the full on both sides. A man who know how to take good care of a women and I've learned many things from you. A woman who know how to please with ease as she made a way for herself because it's new. We both wanted more. Little by little we continue to laugh and play, at times your seriousness appeared the bad boy I say. I never experienced anything like it, it made me want you more. I began to enjoy every moment, drawing ever closer to you. Yes, hard to hold back from loving you. Could this be my true love call, can I yield? For once I could be myself, commit no problem, exchange of passion, and grow with, all seem so right but is it? I'm aware of your situation you put before me and family obligations, just don't know when I could fit you in. There now, we need to talk or do we wait. It's obvious you love and care about it. I admire your reaction you show about everything but it comes a time that we all have to go. We are at a cross road, not for play, will we survive. When we first met we understood, didn't know love will take over just like it should, now it's pulling me. You made this easy for your action speak well, can't you tell. Putting on a show, I love movies this you know, your movie got to go. I'm not stopping in my tracts and wondering if you are coming back. Deep down inside I know you would because I listen to everything you said and knew where you stood. We were not on the same page as before, every time you came through that door, we just out grew each other. Tonight is not surprising you left, because you would rather have your friends around you than me on your back. It's okay cause you would say the same about me but not true, I would rather be with you. So tell me why are you treat me this way? It only can be you would rather have me on my back that way. This is true believe me. This is all we have, thanks for being my friend.

IS IT YOU

Is it you who makes my life so good? Is it you who I see inside of me? Is It you who will be there and true. Is it you who said I'm like you? Is it you who stand in front of me? Is it you who calls and not say I love you? Is it you I kissed and now I miss? Is it you who once said I'm gone and you are here? Is it you who took me in your arms and made me feel warm? Is it you who leave me all alone? Is it you I known and won't crack? Is it you who wants me back? Yes, this is you who words are so slack. Is it you who missing me when I'm not around? Is it you who ride by my house up and down on your way downtown? Is it you who loves to kick it with me and now feeling blues? Is it you who wants me to yourself? Is it you who want me to feel you are here for me? Is it you who leaves me to nowhere? Just stop! I'm not playing these games of yours. If this is you, please do me the favor, open and walk out the door. Don't' look back because I will never say to you again, is it you? You will be looking for my tracks.

STOP THE CALLS

Stop the calling of me on the phone when I tell you to leave me alone. Why do you make me so mad when all you need is someone who is bad? Time and time again, I told you before leave me alone, now you listen! Do you want to be sad? Stop hounding me for the time you lost. If it wasn't for me, you would've been so left out. Your parents are still here and now you acting like you can't hear. Look around you, all your family are grown and on the go. How you see them is not for me. I'm just one, who you shouldn't be with believe me. When I tell you to disappear I mean it, because you are not in the clear.

The noise you make causes me headaches and that's not good. Leave it to you, you would never be understood. Your life is miserable right now this I can tell. While you out there make sure you take your bath. I can smell you from afar, it's not light but dark. That's where you are, you haven't done nothing about it. Take your seat, I will not repeat. You will not come close to me, not sitting at my table or eating out my bowls, you are dry and old. Now distance yourself and this time for good. I'm not just saying it but in every place I stood; not for you but for them who have been in my heart from the start. So the next time before you call, count 1, 2, 3 and only in your dreams will you see me.

TO BE WITH ME

To be with me, I was caught by surprise, if only you could have told me the truth, you would have realized. Hello! You come, coming to me. I was going to do me, because doing me really set me free. You reached me just in time, it made my night blue bright as the stars were shinning so right. My face lit up like glitter, happy to be in your present. Relaxed, welcoming and drawn to you as by crazy glue. My night began as I started to move closer end. No hurry in the world all I could see is you. Peace filled the air, I could only breathe in despair. Your face was like no other, your smile tells me you were ready my brother. That moment was unreal. I can recall me being unstill. When I pulled up, you were standing there, the glow on your face were priceless. I knew it was the start of me and you. Now I have to lock the door, so you could not get through but deep inside we had an arrangement. Let's keep it real. We didn't want to hear words because we knew why we were here, let us enjoy each other as long as we can because tomorrow we have no plans. I know this to be true so do you. I asked for the craziness to go, I didn't need it to make me glow. How I feel is no surprise, when I rise, I rise. You might think I'm wasting my time, but my time is mine. I spread it out like I want too. Could you image us always on the go? Never ask you for what you could not give to another. Satisfaction is what I gain. For I know tomorrow would not be the same. I tell myself this is not what I want, let's keep it real. When I get up this will be gone, do not hold on. Moving forward is what I can see, it just was your turn to be with me.

TIME

Time is the essence of tomorrow that spurs today toward the setting of the sun. It's where the moon hits the horizon at the break of dawn. The flight of a bird as it flies south, the crawl of a snake as it goes into the ground. The pilgrims hurdle together to stay warm. It all takes time, even the coat of human that keep his blood from harm. Let's not forget the glare of the day that causes one to stay and the bare of a tree when it has no leaves, and you sitting in the sun! Remember, the face you made on that cold ass day in hope someone would ride up and get in your way! Here is one more! When longing to hold someone who you know is gone and so on (breathe deep}.

Peace be still, and it seem like everything is going wrong. The hour you gave is now taken away. Daylight you gave is now short. Is this all to be abort? The life we have is never renewed, the tears we cry are many but few. The love you gave have become obsolete. These are your babies, calling you. When all this sadness come upon us, you gave us expensiveness (Christmas), persuasiveness (Black Friday), thankfulness (Thanksgiving), scariness (Halloween), joyfulness (Easter), confusion (Independence Day), don't forget lovingness (Valentine Day). How in the world we can make it out of here! Think positive is what I always hear and said to me, but look around what use to be one now its three. Hold on just a little bit more, there will be something not long at your door. Temptation (Income Tax Return) is what I see. A way to take my mine off my family and me. I will be busy running around, trying to keep a sound mind. When I'm able to breathe snow will be here and now I'm shook because this is the beginning of my book. Time has gone, now the sun arrives just in time.

THE LOVE OF MY LIFE

The love of my life, my love you walked into my life and never left. You came to me, bringing peace and harmony. What a relief! You captured my every wish, my dreams, my tears, my fears and my willingness to live. You became a part of me. You surrounded me by your present of how you entered the room. The smile on your face you brought to me, the light lilt up quietest place in the room, my heart. The realest person I have ever known have penned the tiniest most realistic place there is, I asked myself how could this be for I'm not the one who fall so quickly you see. My life has come with pain, misery, heartaches, trust issues too and now a wall that I vowed to never let no one through. I asked myself "What are you? Who are you? Is this real or are you out for a kill"? I admit you bring light a glow, into my world. A meaning of persistent, wanting and desiring more and more. You fulfill me, complete me, I don't know how, but I'm at my best. I long for you and want to reveal myself to you each and every day. Can this infatuation be for love? I haven't found love at all. I have searched for so long, wishful thinking this could happen to me. I don't know but I may give it a try. I long for attention of a man just to treat me right. I guess I'm going to remain tight. I don't want to see where this will go, I'm not going to put on a show. I going to be myself and allow him to take me on this ride. Time will tell if he is sincere deep down inside. I'm not inviting trouble, looking for the best, maybe we can rest at the end of the day nest. Nest in the way he can feel secure to be who he really is and would see himself in a safe zone. I know he's a man but is he the one for me? I will be there for him, to love, hold, to see things through, I will try something new whatever it takes to make his day! We will laugh, joke, play, hold his hand if that's what is needed, every day. I love to cuddle and kiss, do all the things he deserves because he brings out the best in me, based on how he treats me. I will keep him happy as birds play in trees. It will be a long life for him and me, for I'm not going anywhere. You heard it first and I agree. You are the man in my life, I want you for me and I'm revealing myself to too! The love of my life.

MISSING MORNING

My missing morning happened, when I woke up with him on my mind, like he's an old, old lover of mine. I go to sleep at night, thinking about him as he's been with me all the time. I don't know what's happening to me, when I go out he goes with me. I talk about him, the man I found, he certainly was with me this morning. He doesn't call upon me every day, he reached out to me in his own way. I know he's always there, I can feel him with me and he cares. It's peaceful and good to have him around. It will be so easy for me to fall in love with him. His voice I love to hear, his smile I want to keep it near and his hands I keep a hold, as long as he understands. I have this guy, I want the whole world to know, he makes me feel so sexy about whatever I do or go. Its only him I look forward to waking up with in the morning. He is the most: sexy, sweet, handsome and honest guy I know. What a great combination! If someone would had told me I will meet the most perfect guy, I would've said "you are a lie". Nothing like this has happened to me before, I'm not believing it! Tonight as I lay in my bed, I will be thinking about him and all the things he has said and do, everything seem just right. I know! I believe this is my guy, it has happened to me. Yes, to me, my missing morning.

CLOSURE

Closure for me, as I stand by the opening of the sea, thinking about all the stupidest things that has happened to me. My fight has not been bad but all the people I left, I wanted to make happy is now sad. On my journey is the rules of the game, simple but in order for it to last you have to be put on blast! Protect myself from me because I know how I can be. You're not ready to play in that way, honey none of you can compare or live up to what I needed and wanted to share in that way, do you dare? When my plight goes out I will look only to me, from the beginning I was all I had therefore now stop being sad get over it are you mad? One day I will wake up, right now I'm waiting to be awaken to be happy with new rules of the game. Don't just look to me, for now I'm gone, spend your time wisely. This is my closure precisely.

THAT LITTLE MAN

There was a little man that stayed in the hills. All the people in town called that little man Bill. I often wonder if that was his real name. A man like him who wore a hat like that could never be a shame. When he walked down the street, he walked upright and all the people and things he could see. Bill wasn't little in height or in all his might. He appeared to be so little because he put everyone before he put his own. That's what made Bill so special he had good insight and nothing could pass Bill if it was right. Bill was no ordinary man. Bill had it all, he would give to each and every one even if it was great in cost. The only thing Bill didn't have was a woman who could reach his side and grab him by the hand. Was Bill a kept man? I don't know but when I met Bill, he was the happiest man I've ever seen and the smile he wore was all clean. Bill didn't live long after I had arrived. I look forward to one day seeing Bill again. When I do I'm running to Bill and will greet him with a big fat grin, that little man.

I'M A STRONG BLACK WOMAN

Time tell all, time seen all, a strong black woman will always fall. If you never heard this, well be the first to hear it from me. Every woman wants to be a strong black woman, reality there is only a few that exist as you can see. Define a strong black woman if you can? You have to go back in time, rewind the hardship she experienced inside in order to define a strong black woman mind. Don't get this twisted being educated by the top universities, driving the most expensive car, top of the line clothing, coats and shoes, sneakers too don't make you a strong black woman at all. Don't forget the big house with a pool, all these things are ok, but did you get all these things by following the rules. The code of a strong black woman is now renewed. By far from the truth this we all should know a strong black woman is always on the go. A strong black woman seen it all and still stand tall. The battles she had fought, cries she had, in the cold by night is the choice of her own, a veil she wears to keep her head warm, the stories she kept so long to herself in her eyes it's a story by itself. In the present of a strong black woman you will know, by the way she stands, by the way she enters a room, the glow and the brightness on her face, the air she absorbs leave very little for you. You look around in the room and you see the energy she brings it highlights her in every possible way. This is truthful to say some women get to feeling a certain type of way but she's just a strong black woman who bring a delight to us all. She never compares her to you, for she knows herself, do you? She's the one who will never get recognize because of you. She doesn't care, her struggles are everywhere even among you. You who wants to be a strong black woman who has it all. Who of you will admit the truth of a strong black woman? Only those who are strong and willed at heart, for this is certainly great just because it does not show you are a strong black woman at heart all day. Remember everybody wants to be, only few exist so the next time you see a woman she doesn't need to be define because she wears it every day, never scared to fall, that's what she does. The woman that's now standing or sitting beside you, and making you look small it's okay, not many women can stand beside me, I'm here to tell it all, be at peace with the next strong black woman you see. She carries it all. Yes! I'm a strong black woman and I have shared this with you all.

A NEW CHAPTER

A new chapter always begin with you. Never a dull moment, turns out to be blue. Which one is you? Who's at the door? My heart begins to sing, my smile grew big, and my face started to glow. What a surprise! There was a guy at my front door. What a way to go. Too much for me to sit and not run into the arms of that one. Yes, I know him, I loved him so dearly. He pulled up on me sincerely. It was a surprise. I am happy now, to hear his voice on the outside. If you have to ask yourself if he's here to see me or he, stop playing, really. My feeling is strong my heart pounds for him. I remember my love you came and now you are gone. I refuse to do this anymore. I had hope, on him and no show. I have let go. I'm not second to anyone, even if he promised through a song. It is over, my new chapter just ended in a way that depends on this motivating factor, one of love that what matter.

DAY

What a beautiful day it has been, one that makes you want to sit back and grin. Can you recall a great day like this? A cold glass of ice lemonade, swinging on a pouch as the cars goes by. As you watch in the distance you notice someone walking, old friend comes in and stay for a while. Here comes the sun shinny brightly in the sky, as I turn slightly hits me in the face. My, my, my where is the shade for I'm blinded by the sun this day.

HELLO

Hello, hello, hello! I'm talking to you, you and you! You remember when I was young. I use to walk downtown with my head hung. My body so tight, any cars that pass would all most end up in the grass. The women would stare and the girls would wish, I knew then I shook. That was me, 28, 22, 36 what a figure to have. To my haters you have always hated, even back then you couldn't relate. Presently, you all have grown up, as I look at you all I am still in my zone. No need to get an attitude, I have always loved me and everything about me. I have always talked so gracious about me. You didn't know that because you never got to know me, you stopped at my body. Some of you will not agree or understand, it's okay man but do I care. No, I don't because the smiles on your face, the things that were said and all the comment you made that is still running in your head is all to fake. Wake up my people now it's too late. Mentally fighting all my life, I just did not know it was me I was fighting for. Thanks mom for being there for me spiritually, you made me see when all others was against me from the old to the young, I didn't fit in nor did I belong. You see I don't need to be guessing and carrying on because of where I'm standing, I can tell you so long. Right now you are looking at me like I said something wrong, If I did, this stage is mine and you just run. From now on I say whatever I want, since I have all your attention, it's the same as back then, you all are haters and still you can't defend! I just did. Hello!

RESPECT

When a man decides to call you out of your name "Baby". You never met him before or talked to him long, beside saying hello. Every time he talks to you, he calls you baby, sexy, or sweetheart. He's interested in getting to know you and he's over 55. The conversing start:

He: When are you going to let me come and see you baby?

She: Why would I? You don't know how to respect a woman.

He: Yes I do.

She: Day 1, I introduced myself to you. I corrected you when you called me sweetheart on that first day. You have noticed I have not responded to many of your messages. The messages I had responded to you turned right around and call me sexy, or baby. It's been several times I've asked you to call me by my name. I know you knows it but it's always the same. I'm not a baby as you can see, I'm a woman who ask to be respected, humbly.

He: Okay

Her: Thanks

He: What are you doing this weekend?

He: No response

He Hello

He: Good Morning

Her: Good Morning

He: How are you doing today?

He: Good Morning Belinda

Yes, he missed the point. He refused to hear that's okay. I have myself dear, respect.

GONE

Gone! Get out of my life. Are looking for something to read? I'm still writing my story therefore you can have a seat and watch from afar. This is my life in this jar. You must find it appealing, I thank you if you do. The one thing I want to ask you. Always be a woman about it when you need to know. Just ask, it really not that hard. Life is too short to play games, go straight to the point. Why stress yourself? You can talk behind my back. I will not even know because the people you run with I don't even know. You are, what you are to me invisible. A thought on a distance memory. Get a life and continue on, I forgot you don't have one, so gone.

THE SCENT I SMELL

What's this scent I smell? I don't know it, but if it fills this room we are doom. Everyone carries a scent. Some wears it well, all scent have a smell. What scent do you have or do you know? Some have many scents because they are always on the go. Those who have one scent sometimes wish they had more. Some have more scent than they can carry, you can easily smell them being in a hurry. Some have scents that linger. Some have scents that make you sneeze man or woman, you want to say please! Have you come across a scent that just carries? This scent you just want to breathe it in and hold it within. All scents are important for it tell who you are. Whether you are clean or dirty that scent depend on the scent you carry. Don't go smelling yourself now, I can see you somehow. Look over to the next person you are beside and see their expression, the scent they smell now inhale.

REFLECTION

Mirror, mirror on the wall, what I see is a picture of it all. Here I stand in front of it, just to recall what I see was long ago written before me. A reflection of the past to highlight the way and it's not how we see it going on today. It's the opposite we are getting paid. This is my mirror day. As the mirror hangs on the wall when I walk by it, I began to ball. What is it I see, many shades of lights appear before me, I'm in my dance clothes, that's shear. All the people sitting around chilling with no words or sound, just wanting for me to take the floor. I do as soon as I walk through the door. The music sound great, the DJ is playing my favorite welcoming song, it put me right in the mood, where I stood. I began to dance, dance, and dance right on through for all for you! Time have passed, many have dropped off and I can see myself in the mirror. My reflection as I created this vision for everyone to enjoy once more. I'm in the moment of starting to tell you my story from the beginning to the end as I reflect looking in the mirror I saw, my reflection.

MISERY LANE

Here I sat on this log, I'm letting go of it all. It might not be a lot to you but now you are few. I have seen good days and bad days all for a while. It's time to put it all in a pile. I will let you know what's bothering me for today I want to breathe easily. People always come and go, some just don't show and I don't know. I want a little more, I'm tired of showing everyone the same door. Listen careful and take it for what it's worth, I am simple, simple as can be. If you miss out then you have join me, misery lane.

NOW

Today is the day, that you accept me now, right here where I stand. I stand before you today like I am. Tomorrow I will be standing another way. Listen to me, I will admit one day soon you will be standing where I just stood, accept me now.

ME, MYSELF AND I

Me, myself and I, what do you say and why? Nothing is coming forth, when I think of me, myself and I. This is how I'm writing it today, why bother no one seem to care anyway. I do because me, myself and I have many plans to follow through, I'm not giving up until we have completed all on the list. Each day I add one more to be open up and even the score. This one is new, it's not just around the corner you have to reach out and connect, breaking all sorts of barriers when you finished you are a winner. First you have to be polite to all you meet, then converse to find interest and you can share then pray no one knows you are there. Hard to break, characters you find, you put on airs to just reach the blind, blind to other influence about you. It's a shame when you don't mix with none, only me, myself and I. Most are shallow minded about many things. They look to others to be entertained, it's not due to their own but because of the one you cannot see, that's who bothers me. Being careful as always as I move forth for tomorrow is another day by choice. I will keep being true to me because one I will have to admit I found myself by my own encounters as I pleaded for me and the result is me, myself and I.

A FRIEND OF MINE

It was not far in time, when you became a friend of mine. Each and every day we could not wait to talk on the phone, with the glass in one hand. We would laugh and grin about the funniest things and time would fly right on by. We had the best discussions, talking fast then slow until our jaw were sore. We had so much to share, for life was an open road and we both were in despair. We learned from each other as those day went by, how exciting it was just to know each other. We shared many thoughts and intention, man if we were in school we would have been put in detention. We unraveled and solved mysteries, for that wasn't all, we did it having the best time as we both sometimes dropped the ball. We would sit and watched people going and coming. I where here, you where there, we couldn't imagine not being together, always made it happen anywhere. Somewhere back in time we lost the readiness to share, things got complicated and put on a shelf. We promised to revisit it soon but the more time past, it looks doom. I will always consider you a friend of mine even though you left me long ago back in time. You don't mention me anymore, a friend of mine.

LIFE

As I ponder over life, many situations run to my mind. I stop to wonder, caught up and seemingly couldn't move forward. I managed after a while, putting it to rest. I only wish things could have turned out better or for the best. Can you control your life even without a manual or remote? You can always fix the things in life that need to be fixed before it's too late. Life brings many disappointments setting you up as bate. Stop if you can relate, to life.

Children are our biggest joy in life, always pleasing to you, making the worst situation into a perfect one. That's what a parent suppose too do. Outsider approach, you give everything you can, who don't want it, to have it together is not in their plan. A perfect life it would seem but not for that one, who only see their way to glean. Taken for granted each and every day and its okay, but when you leave you will wish you had stayed. You have come to care any way.

A different path you are now walking, shoes we all have to fill not by choice but at will. Do you finally close the door on it all? Yes, for now, the choice you made was your own and I'm gone. To find me is not so hard, I know who I am and not a retard. Insecurities I don't have, look at me. No, here look at me, I know you see. True to my word I have to be, life. Life for you and me.

I want to sow a seed and let it be, no way this life turns for me. I want you to remember, I dropped seeds everywhere. Some will make it, some you will cut out, but one will last and break through, now you are anxious are you. One day you will grow up, your emotions will take over, silly me you say but you may, you earn it, now have your day.

Some may ask, do I settle? Some say get in where you fix in, hardly! There is no perfect situation. Life can be hurtful, disappointing, selfish, stupid and even crazy. We all deal with this life we live. What make you so important? Oh it's my turn, good. I'm who I am. Let me show you. You feel great, do you not? Are you happy? Yes, I am. Where do you want to go? Nowhere. Are you at peace? Yes! What do you want to do? Many things but not without you. Are you hungry? No, you feed me. Are you wanting for things you don't have? Yes, only because I don't have it. Let me show you, how to get that too.

Encouragement means a lot, it never going to bring you down. One day someone will recognize your worth. Family knows you and it's okay, others will come to know you at the end and when they do you walk away. You leave it all but one day you will take your stand in your place in the life race. Hard pill to swallow, life.

A WOMAN

A blessing truly, delightful always, wonderfully searching, and a brilliant gift to one that deserves. What! What! You know. Do you have one or desire one? Did you take it for granted? Do you wish you had one? Did you appreciate it, when you had it? I know, you didn't know how to keep it. Grow up! Life is short. Please! Are you a teaser? Look to your left and to the right, do not look down, sorry you did and I see you. It's nothing there, but a very small brain. Thinking you want to be satisfied for the moment, let's move on. Every great gift comes with a warranty. You can choose to purchase it, extend it, limit or unlimited warranty, you settled and let it go, you know. If you buy it, you determine how long you want it to last, do you not? Now your gift is all wrapped up. It's doing everything you want it to do. You use it in ways you didn't think was possible. It's just what you wanted. Years come and go, it's your gift for sure, you are still using it. It breaks you fix it, if it became misplaced, you found it. You searched hard, never giving up until you recovered it. It's your heart and you cherished it. It can never be replaced. The funniest thing, just like that warranty you choose not to buy, when it breaks, you can't fix it. Now you wished you made the right choice at the time, you didn't, guess what! Good written. You know what I mean. Who of you have never regretted not buying a warranty with an expensive purchase? That's when things tend to go wrong. Now you're searching, putting it out, throwing it down, breaking it, cursing it, only uses it when you find a need to do so, if you can but try. Don't fool yourself, a warranty is good to have in these days. Would you agree? So pick a woman, make her the happiest woman around. She will be your pride and joy, your warranty. Remember a woman.

A NEW BEGINNING

A new beginning start by saying hello, thank-you, you're welcome, how's your day or just a friendly smile and you be on your way. It attracts, make you stop, pause for a minute or just don't see at all. It's happening the change is within you. Now, you become well-spoken of, it's encouraging to you. It could have skip or slipped or pass you right by. The choice is yours, you get what I mean guy.

The objective is to always be open, not close nor put up unnecessary walls and bars. Come on for I am not from Mars. We all make mistakes. Why are you looking at me up and down? For we are all clowns. Whether we are happy, sad or mad, a new beginning of something that I haven't had. Things could have been done better on both of our part, one stops the other want to depart.

Looking back on the hands of time, I'm set in my ways and you have a mind. We have to be flexible, learn how to bend and relax because adjusting is part of life being played. All this is good and I've said it many times before, I have kids and I don't want any more. We are at this point now, it's time to move on and mate.

Days now goes by fast, I want to keep up, up with being me and feeling free and glad. Free to act, express the way I want and yet I'm being me all along. Simple things in life, I enjoy. A phone call, a hello, how are you doing, are you enjoying your day is all a concern but not in a certain way, just to jump start my new day. Life is short, we have to live and the last thing on my mind is the past. No bad memories for me, don't even bring it up for it's a time for everything, today is not one.

Now you have my full attention and you're wondering what to do. You want to decide whether I'm true. Games I don't play, drama is no more my concern, I have spread my wings and now making a dash because it burns. The door is open, ha, ha, you see, I'm walking, it can't be me. I have held on to every word you said, for I am simple, you see. I have made your life my world. A new beginning is the beginning we wanted at first, I never received it and I allowed someone else make it worst. Breathe!

My new beginning, I will not let go, I will fight for it I know. My new beginning starts now and it's here. I'm going to explore it all the more. I'm going to make it here, near to me. I'm going to hold on to it and never let it go because my new beginning is here you see, me!

LIVE

When a flower began to bloom, it's amazing even when it pebbles start to fall. Seize that moment, while the flower is in bloom for every moment you enjoy because when it becomes old the foliage is everywhere. You slowly pick it up, one by one, still holding on to some. For time tells it all, you never know how short or when it gets cut. So live.

Think about this flower, when your words bring tears and smiles together. Your writing is so real and now reality has come for you to take your place in an open space. You have no time to waste, let's be hast and fade away together. A keeper desires a reaper just like a flower that bloom in it's on time, it's a keeper amazing, now live.

What

Five years have passed, wishing you had come to pass, holding on to strings, that had a bigger picture in my head. Down the drain, it had persuaded my mind to embrace time only to find out it was your dream and not mine. It was all going on in the heart, I was suckled and made no part. I cried, feeling the tear as it rolls down my face, I realized, I was only used for bait.

It wasn't long I met another one after promising myself distancing is where I belong. Conversing with each other on a regular basis, I begin to open up without any traces, upfront and all, I placed it out there and now it's on my terms if I fall. No longer was I the woman I used to be, I had gain more respect by being me, for myself than anyone could see.

We all have dreams that cause ones to stumble and looks around and you plunder. A forced to open, no respect was gain I lost that day and would never be the same. My heart was ripped out of me, my legs you pulled apart. Humility was inside of me, the pain I bottled up, once more I was just out there all messed up.

As I think back I became a slave that was on her back, I cried and I cried, I also grew. This day forward I knew exactly what to do. Many harsh words given to me, I took it all in strive to push me forward and not die even though it hurt. It was not easy I realize my worth.

In the morning as I was riding in my car, I received a text, an apology. I didn't need one nor did I wanted it but I said nothing. Fear and nervousness I became, how in the world could I win. I went on to record this because I knew I was not the only one. This fight can never be won. My heart goes out to everyone that have gotten something from these words of mine, It's just goes back to the days of a song, a journey I'm on, not by myself. I picking up strays all by myself I have to wonder what had happened to me, am I not worthy to become the one for me, for my safety at risked, my net is down.

I talked to myself and the more I talk the more strength I gain. The woman that reside within me, have changed. I became glad to have her on her side it was nothing I couldn't tell her when I begin talking I became tired. Never be sad for me, for I have regained my strength you see. When I now look back I put up a fight to move on. Now my tunnel is bright, I am a glad sister and can stand tall for my past is behind me and my plan lies before me and my worth says it all.

IN YOUR MIND

It hurts to think you want to rough me up, when you are just like water that hit the stone as the wind blows causing it to spill or slashes against the rocks then hits the sand. There's nothing left but a little moist that quickly dry up, disappear. Really!

It hurt to think you want to rough me up, when you are just like a breeze that comes down through the tree leveling houses and everything that get in its way. It stood for a while and shook as many as it could, see how it passes on and now it takes only the leaves because it could. Who are you fooling? Wow!

It really hurts me to know you want to rough me up, when you are just like a cub that wonders, looking for prey knowing the lion is near, stalking, pouncing and waiting to see if your success will be on me, you rise and you die. You will never give up because in your mind, it's always that time. You just can't let go of yesterday, for today and tomorrow it will bring. Are you struck?

Release yourself and move on realizing each day holds its own. Changes will come but for now embrace the moment be yourself and let it take you away. Only then will you begin to enjoy the water still runs but just not fast but slow.

When the breeze become refreshing to your soul. It's time to exhale without fear, gradually it will appear. It's a wonderful thing. Yes! A cub can be just as powerful as it was years ago. The hurt lies with you in your mind. It's right in time. Smiling.

MY BROTHER

If ever I tell you about a man, I think of my brother, the coolest man I know. Full of life, laughter, peace toward all and none other, a good friend. Many didn't understand him and me, he knew this to be true, what appears to be underserved to some, was deserving of it all and he was free. Free to live, act, anyway he wanted, a come and go person. Always pleasant and lending a hand, when one was in need, he was the man. Never a dull moment with him. He would be the life of the party and didn't care what nobody would think. He forever had my back, all I had to do was wavy, blink or throw my hand back. He's always around looking and watching me. He's a special guy to me. He would get on the dance floor and dance, dance until no more, for he now wanted a drink. He wasn't a selfish man, he would offer to buy drinks, for he knew what to do and think. I gave him the title my brother because I began to value him and our relationship grew. He was sincere and true always looking out for you and that was me too. I love my brother this you could see. He knew me well and still wanted to be with me! My brother was injured back early this year in 2020. It surely been hard for I miss him dear. He no longer recognizes me anymore and this hurts my heart and I will always remember my brother who played with me in heart and that special part. The part of my life I never really had a brother who cared and shared his dreams and inspirations with me. I went to his bed side just to be with him, for I left him a part of me, a picture he could see each time he wakes up, it would be me he would see. I think of my brother now once and a while, for I know he's there even if he doesn't remember me, but he will smile. It makes me happy he's still alive. He's doing the best of what he can in the mean while. I know one day in the future to come, we will be back together again as one, not as before but better when all is done. I pray for him and his family for I know the challenges are hard. The time my brother and me had was so short, I hoped for more time being together with my bother than now out way the time we are apart, my brother.

This book is the inspiration of all the relationships of the past. As I gain the momentum to express and relate to an unforeseen environment that have filtered into a society beyond all moral thinking. The world of unsettling in thoughts and behavior, where one could grow as they choose, with little or none to guide. It embraces the world through my eyes and hold no fundamental values of letting go as I seek and never finds. This book of inspiring words and poems are dedicated to my mother, Josephine Sears with love.

The End

www.ingramcontent.com/pod-product-compliance
Ingram Content Group UK Ltd.
Pitfield, Milton Keynes, MK11 3LW, UK
UKHW041915190726
13854UKWH00003B/1262